I.D.

Philip Gross was born in 1952 in Delabole, Cornwall. His father was a Displaced Person from Estonia; his mother was Cornish. After studying English at Sussex University, he worked in publishing and libraries before moving to Bristol. He won a Gregory Award in 1981 and the National Poetry Competition in 1982; in 1989 he received a major Arts Council bursary. He now divides his time between writing (poetry, novels and plays), work in schools and colleges, and his family.

I.D.

Philip Gross

faber and faber
LONDON · BOSTON

First published in 1994
by Faber and Faber Limited
3 Queen Square London WC1N 3AU

Photoset in Sabon by Wilmaset Ltd, Wirral
Printed in England by Clays Ltd, St Ives plc

A CIP record for this book is available from the British
Library

ISBN 0-571-17235-0

2 4 6 8 10 9 7 5 3 1

Acknowledgements

Acknowledgements are due to the following magazines and anthologies: *Blue Nose Anthology*, *The Green Book*, *London Magazine*, *London Review of Books*, *Poetry Book Society Anthology 2*, *Poetry Review*, *The Rialto*, *Spectator*, *Stand*, *Times Literary Supplement*, *Where She's Tender* (Spacex Gallery), *Writers on the Storm* (Avon Poets on the Gulf War) and the Cardiff Festival poetry competition.

Several poems in this collection originate from *A Game of Henge*, *Grace Notes*, *Road Movies* and other collaborations with the improvisatory music group Vanilla Allsorts.

Contents

Fillings

It wasn't so much the stones
I loved, aged nine.
It was the word *archaeology*.

It was books pocked with diagrams
like pawprints round the bins
in last night's snow;

they showed circles complete
with the things that weren't there:
post-holes, lost stones –

like the scene of the crime,
the victim's parting gesture
plotted on the pavement;

or the files the dentist kept on me
and everyone, living and dead
cheek by jowl in his metal safe.

Like the shudder and thrill
when I read in the paper:
'*they identified him by his teeth.*'

Nocturne with Glue

Listen, it's almost
not a sound at all —
the sound of one a.m.
It's peaceful
as the glaze of water
idling
just above the waterfall.

Somebody jets by
with his sun roof open
to the dark. He leaves a trail
of disco funk
like broken glass. I know
he'll have a sticker: HONK
IF YOU HAD IT LAST NIGHT.

The binbags are out,
sleeping rough again,
one with its mouth wide open.
A thin finicky fox
looks up
from its spillage of takeaway cartons.
It spares half a glance for me.

2

half for the thin boy
by the bus stop going nowhere.
He droops with the weight
of his head in his hands. He sways
as if combing the gutter
for something he lost but
what? He jerks round

with a whimpering growl,
he crouches, he snuffs deep
from his polythene bag.
It's a crumpled ego, a speech-
bubble saying WAITROSE.
The fox shifts gear
smoothly, into fight-and-flight.

Beyonders

They live like us,
amongst us. Think of the years
they watched our houselights
from a distance. Now they're here

they'll always leave 40 watts wasting
on the stairwell, or an anglepoise
downcast on its desk at midnight.
It's the same with their eyes:

you can see the bare filament
quivering, you can hear the brittle whine
like one mosquito in a lampshade
that puts them in mind

of the millions more that rise
out of swamp pools in veils
of cheap nylon that snag on your skin.
For a moment they're back

in the old beyond. Then
Sorry, they'll say,
a bit too casually,
I was miles away . . .

*

They speak like us but
as if schooled in it later in life.
Their mother tongue is silence

only, when it falls,
each looks away.
Every one has a different dialect;

how can they hope
to reconstruct the histories they need?
Of a land where someone's ancestors

thrashed their grey herds to and fro
beneath the skirts of mother Winter,
ducking most of her wallops.

Of a thousand-mile
branch line leading nowhere
but a barbed-wire gate. Of days

chunked from the frost
and thawed by body heat . . .
(They have cold-burns to prove it.)

Of some millennial
construction project sinking into bog
as steadily as it grows . . .

All lies. Besides,
they never speak of it.
Don't ask me how I know.

*

What won't they do
for a bit of your warm regard?

They'll take any amount and mail it home

except there's no address
and no one there

to take it in, not now or ever.

*

Heard the one about the Boy
Lost in the Snow?
Ask any of them. They'll tell you.
Winter granted him one gift:
he could not die, or grow.

His tale dogged them to the city.
He could be roughing it out there now.
That could be his shadow
on any curtain, no matter
how carefully closed.

How sad, you say, polite.
They'll snort: *The little bastard.*
Once let him in
and you'll never be warm again.
(But a good story, no?)

*

Some sit it out
in bedsits. Most assimilate
hungrily. Some of them excel
in the art of forgetting till not
even they can tell
themselves from me or you.

I knew one who would sparkle and glow
at all the best addresses.
Only, when the last
guest left, the hostess
found her carpet printed with a cross-
pattern tread of mud and snow

and nothing she could do would shift it.

Shift

In the city of No
it's one-way, lights at Stop or Caution, peristalsis in the belly
of the beast, the traffic flow . . . *Move on*

through the precincts of Nor,
past coffee shops where ladies of a certain age meet lives they
never had, comparing what they never wore. *Move on*

down the high street of Nope
past street-squatters in battle fatigues, with inflammable eyes,
with lean dogs given just enough rope. *Move on*

round the ring road of Nay.
Billposters flense a huge grin, barbers mowing lines of shaving
foam and skin. It falls like tickertape. *Move on*

past the dockside at Null.
Bags, drowned fish, condoms, years float by beneath the
mugger's eye, the rag-and-bone cry, of the blackback gull.
Move on, move on.

In the pool halls of Nil
a lean lad stretches like a leopard out along his cue. Crunch of
balls like the bones of the kill . . . *Move on.*

When the city of No
shuts one eye for the night, with a sound of trouble breathing,
when a sudden doorway steams as if it's all about to blow

don't wait to be told. Just go.

Bonfire Night

As they're dumped, so they lie.
She's a soggy-damp mattress,
all puckers and lumps. He's her guy

with a head full of paper. His sack-
cloth skin itches them both
and his finger-twigs scratch

where she's tender. He's stiff
in all the wrong places. Whoosh
from next door's garden and a whiff

of cordite . . . Always out of sight,
those oohs and ahs. Strike, strike
a match. The bloody thing won't light.

Him

He's the great I AM.
He's a pushy little jerk.
He's a bloke who rolls his sleeve up
when he gets to work.
He's an ageing pup
who only knows one trick:
how to sit up and beg.
Pretty dumb. Tock, tick,
he's a homemade bomb
none too accurately primed.
He's a maestro on his rostrum
trying to beat time:
dum-dum-dum. He's a purple-
hooded monk whose vow
to be good lasts as little
as a quarter of an hour.
He's an actor playing Hamlet
in the bedroom farce.
He's a boy stood up blushing
in front of the class
trying not to cry,
not to break and run to mum.
(The taller he grows
the bigger baby he becomes.)

He's a shaky-shaky rattle.
He's a marching drum.
He's a soft-headed bullet:
dum dum . . .

Flits

Black cab under the arches
ticking, lights killed,
engine drumming its fingers,
sparks flicked from the driver's
window like a lit fuse.
Black cab under hire

with its meter alive
like a sanctuary lamp:
red numbers twitch
in their sleep like dogs;
at after-midnight rates
they dream quick. I'm waiting

to see someone emptied on the street
in a downpour of send-offs
like the last New Year's Eve
of the century. Or creep
downstairs with one
case, the click of the latch

a loaded gun
cocked at too many years
of silence. I'm still waiting.
Is he out already
in the back seat of the black cab
clinching deals of love or money

13

or alone with the thrill
of watching time tot up
to his last p?
Then he'll tap the glass
and shake his wallet empty
and be gone. Black cab,

are you waiting for me?

Figure in Landscape: China Clay

A Desert Father might have been at home here:
acres of quartz slag that give to the boot
    with a masculine crunch.
    The soft stuff's gone,
pulled in grey-silky bolts, folded neat
in square settling-ponds down the valley.

No end to it: the moorside overflows
with grit cleanly as caustic soda,
    like the top hat
    plundered by a conjuror
with both hands shovelling a froth
of doves up, half-frightening, white as this

or the light of the mind. It's a Zen
monk's garden with one boulder left
    in rigorous asymmetry,
    the texture of fudge
made with ground glass, and concentric
ruts of tyre-treads raked around it.

There's a breathing, like surf at the brink
of things, quite close, rising, falling, and yes,
    here's a fifty-foot gulch
    and a sandblast of spray.
A swivel-cannon with a throbbing hose,
way down, is stropped to piss the cliff away

while in his sentry-box one living soul
sits his shift out. Swills of froth
    make deltas round him.
    He might be a deserter
from the family this Bank Holiday, a father
to whom this place has come to seem like home.

A Guest of the Atlantic

Blame the state I'm in this morning on the waitress,
her and her surfer, all night in the other attic room.

I'd passed them on the stairs. Her landed merman,
he looked like someone come to do the plumbing, or his mate,

with a six-pack toolkit. Then it was the steady scrape
of his voice through the wall, hers demurring, just enough

to keep us all up. When at last my toothmug started
rattling on the basin, all the crying-out-loud

was his. Then, quite soon, running water in the pipes
that connected us. Then his snores. Was she there at all?

*

Somewhere down the line I dozed and I was dreaming
I was Cornwall, varicose with rivers, cramped
in an armlock of sea. I was a crumpled map

full of words that were me too but what
did they mean? Praze-an-Beeble, Zelah, Perranzabuloe . . .
Then there was dawn picking holes in the curtains.

I woke numb all down one side. I tried not to move
as if I could put off what came next, the pain
that would sew my two halves back together,

pins-and-needles like the screel of rooftop gulls.

*

The surf was mixing concrete all night.
There's the beach, damp-dark, new-laid,
spoiled with footprints already.
The wind flaunts straight into the waves
which start to smoulder – overheating brakes
or a tyre in a skid or hot fat

nearing flashpoint. The surfers are up.
Reduced to their own silhouettes
in wetsuits they range out along a swell,
cave-painted hunters, watchful less
of the prey, which is vicious but slow,
than of each other. Who will strike the killing blow?

*

In black and white, trim-pinnied, she's serving again.
There's a coffee-dregs look in her eyes.
She drops two rounds of post
beside my breakfast in a silver toast rack:

c/o *The Atlantic Hotel. Please forward.*
Hungry for a *Missing You*
or two I slit them then, to prove
I'm free, let them lie, and read the window:

waves rule thick smudged lines;
the surfers' heads are punctuation
with no words. They break all at once,
all but one. He's waiting, days,

nights, for the biggie, the one
with his name lettered through it
like rock, the one that – since Chaos
Theory's all we've got to go on –

could be stirring in the womb
of the Atlantic now, conceived
by the cough of an outboard motor
somewhere in the Gulf of Mexico.

Wind Farm and Sky Dishes

The hillside's just made an emergency landing,
turbo-props cut, the blades freewheeling
    as it taxies in

with a low thwarted sound. We still don't know whether
to run out like innocent natives to welcome it. Better
    not. We draw the curtains

on a skyline restless as the cut of gull-
wings melling round a gulp of outfall.
    Old Stan-boy, though,

he keeps an eye on it all hours, especially by moonlight.
He sees tumblers, freaks with three white-tighted
    thighs each, like on Manx stamps.

Or he's back on Bude beach, shortest in a thin
red-eyed, white-faced and blue-lipped line
    abreast, with tinfoil spinners

clutched head-high as if to exorcise the wind.
Or he just lets the sight bemuse him,
    better than the reps

he traps when he can on his doorstep; he demands
the whole patter. (Look, it slices as it blends
    as it minces the sky.)

It's better than the world that trickles down
the wires to his screen, looking worn
        and thready as the sheets

in a holiday let; the sets of sitcoms shudder
when gales twang the aerial. We stay indoors
        more and more. Each cottage

holds its begging bowl up to the sky,
to the one fixed point they all watch; they
        know something's coming

that's still nothing to the naked eye.

Downhometown
(Delabole)

Houses littered down the roadside
like some lorry's shed load . . .

Here's where it's at, without the option.
Stacked blue plastic crates

glimpsed through the window of the British Legion
                                                    hall . . .
Last weekend's fête,

a buff handbill slapped up on the village
like an order to evict . . .

On the forecourt of the shut-up shop
the odd half-dozen scuff their heels.

One stares up the road, then down,
and can't decide. One considers the kerb,

leans his weight on a lamppost and kicks
the place as if it's jammed;

if he could just dislodge it everything
would light up and start humming.

The girls have memories already;
they name names from school,

who's in the army, who's in jail.
'What, *Gavin*? Him?' – 'The quiet ones,

they're the worst.' – 'Yeah, did you ever
see his eyes?' They stop

as if I'm nothing, passing,
but a slight chill in the air.

They don't look at each other but,
together, at the place I might have been.

All Night Breakfast

Eyes, your eyes in the rear view mirror . . .
Red and white head and tail lights
opening to slip you in, soft as a sigh,
as the dial tips ninety. TAKE A BREAK:

and there's a service station, beaming
like a bright idea. Pull over. Pee. Tuck in
to the All Night Breakfast, or nothing.
Someone in the kitchen sweeps and sweeps

like a record that won't reject.
The till-girl sits in her small tent of light,
the one nurse on the ward.
You sit down by the window and stare through

to a dimmer-lit lounge. Departures.
TIXƎ, the door says in the script
of that country and there's always one
of the other-side people gazing back

as they wait for their flights to be called.
Red, white: outside, the runway lights
converge. Engines shudder to go.
Take a break. It's no distance at all.

He Went that Way

A shot-gun cartridge
stomped in the rutted-up mud . . .

it's not. It's a throw-away
flick-lighter, out of gas.

Zigzag tyre-treads
have snarled up the verge

as if the whole damn lay-by
couldn't hold a man like him,

whoever he was, out of sight
up the road now, out of mind.

He'll be talking to thin air
signing himself on as *Fozzie Bear*,

locking in to anyone
who's passing on his wavelength

like a non-stop chat-show
or a séance. He's a greyish haze

where the road impacts on a horizon
as straight-down-the-line

as a government health warning.
If this place remembers him

it's as dust and a burnt smell
settling. Wagtails tap-

test the puddles for damage.
You can see the whole wide sky

in a dented hubcap
and the clouds are heavy bruising

working to the surface
slowly, slowly.

Quite what's happened,
it's too soon to say.

Life in the Slow Lane

9.30: everybody
with a life to go to
has got up and gone.
What's left slows down.

An old man, winded
by the long hill home,
pulls up a wall
to scan the morning

like a job half done.
Here comes a mother
leashed to the snow-
booted plod of her toddler.

He's a one-child
cul-de-sac: the prints
he peters out
from puddles are a track

he's always coming to the end of.
The wind tweaks his ear.
He begins to move and creak.
There's a grey dog,

louche and sidelong, no-one's
chum, off at a trot, diagonal,
to pass by always
on the other side

. . . while I
try to quicken and clip
my footsteps like the doctor
on the long-stay ward

who knots his tie
and his smile crisply.
Otherwise
who could tell him from the patients?

Walkman

The girl with the Walkman
screws her eyelids shut

as if to keep the sound in.
Bass rattles her bones;

the treble leaks out
like the sweeping-up of crockery

when the couple upstairs
have had one of their tiffs.

(When they make it up later
in their rusty bed

it's like a woodwork-
for-beginners class

knocking up a pig pen
with a pig already in it.)

January 15th, 1991

So here I am, walking
downhill on a winter morning
so still I can hardly believe,

walking in sunlight, light
and empty as the empty street
or the word *war*, when

with a wheeze like a milk float
a compressor kicks in up the lane.
One man coils red tangle-tape

spike to spike. Another
watches, while their mate
in the teddy-bear earmuffs

stands to his drill,
high-hunched as if taking a pee
on a freezing day.

Each peck pogoes him stiffly
backwards inch by inch
leaving the concrete rucked

like vertebrae, the fossil
of an as-yet-nameless
armoured reptile lying unbelievably

somehow just beneath the surface.

This Train Does Not Stop Here

Blink: shuffled packs
of housebacks. Wheelie bins
in binyards with NO BALL GAMES.
Three whippety lads
squint up and cup their smokes

like lookouts. Blink:
there's a kid's bike slewed
on a verge, a Buddhist
prayer wheel, ticking,
and no child in sight. Blink:

stiff white plastic chairs,
two to each patio, sit side
by side and empty
with the Sunday paper
making fantails. Short

exposures, courtesy
of Inter City 125:
brief lives opened-and-shuttered.
I flip through them time
and again for a sight

of the boy who lost years
on windy platforms waiting
for the quickening, the twitch
of a signal wire . . .
Then blinked and missed

the name-plate in the blur,
the faces peeling past
like a photo-booth strip,
its gloss not dry yet
so it came off on my fingers.

Mugshot

I've got the prints —
like computer-enhanced
blow-by-blow-ups
of one in the crowd

they can't account for;
like the space probe's
strip-search of Saturn.
I can't deny

they're my writing,
the lopsided lines
on that face. How can
my right-hand man

not have known what the left
was doing?
When they smile
not quite together,

one eye's wide, *who —
me?* One's hooded
like a kept hawk.
When they speak,

their joint communiqués
can be spin-doctored
left or right.
How can the centre hold

while maps of half of Europe
hit the shredders?
Men whose mugshots
may one day appear

on War Crimes lists
or postage stamps, depending,
weigh the chances
that the age demands a man

to stand – judge,
jury, executioner –
and say the word.
The word is: *me*.

Midi

Poor mad-dog Englishman,
he's lost his bearings and all sense of time.

It's the heat. Mid-day, mid-life,
he's like the gnomon of a sundial
on the bald lawn of his *gîte*.

All round him, insect cogwheels
shrill on, powered by the sun.

Whole fields are glittered
with polythene cloches like swarf
from a metal-grinder's bench.

He's nailed to the spot
like the cats in the village

laid flat by the heat
as the church on its hill
beats out twelve in a hurry

like a dinner gong.
Then he sights it: a pom-pom of cloud

that always sits just there
on that horizon, even on the clearest day.
Breath of the *Centre Nucléaire*.

That's north. The sun's straight up.
The sundial tells no time at all.

The End of the End
of the Pier Show

Undressing alone
in a room I won't remember
I'm joggling on one leg

trying to kick crumpled jeans
like a slobbery dog
away. They won't let go,

then drop and won't
lie down, but keep the form
of crotch and thigh,

still warm, as if
I'd peeled myself off neatly.
Skin. Face. Smile.

It's the end of the show
and in some back-
stage hole

a mirror
framed in bare bulbs stares
across the dressing-table, blank

as a poker fiend's face.
The name on the posters
has let himself out

by the back way
locking up behind. Beneath
the planks beneath his feet

foam sucks on girders.
Anglers hunched in a row
don't turn as he passes,

punters queuing all night for a show
that's already sold out
and no one told them.

At the passport-photo booth
he tries the slot
out of habit, just in case

there's a face to spare.
He frisks himself
for 10p. There's always his friend

for a moment like this –
the ghost, his friend
the ghost in the Speak Your Weight machine.

The Book of Doh Noh

He was his own
bad joke, and told it faithfully
for ninety years.

He was old from the very beginning.

Some called him a sounding gong
of wisdom; some,
an old tin can. Opinions are,

by their nature, divided.

By the end he was perfectly
childish: *Knock knock*. Who's there?
Doh Noh. Doh Noh who?

Nor do I. Ask me another.

*

No answer
and the door was locked. He sat.

He sat all night. Next day
he thought: *that's my door!*

And the third day:
                                    where
did I put the key?

On the fourth he thought:
there is no key. On the fifth:

there is no door.
On the sixth: *there is no me.*

On the seventh day
he spoke: 'Come in?'

It swung open.

                              *

If you see a man beating a donkey
think: what is beating the man?
It may only be a bluebottle
but tell that to the donkey . . .

If you see a man driving an army
think: what is driving the man?
It may be he had a father
with a bluebottle of his own.

If you see a bluebottle,
think. You could swat it,
just like that. But who can tell
what mayhem might ensue?

                              *

Somehow the paint would not stick.
It just dribbled away

leaving a little vacancy
much the shape of the sage

who sat smiling, perfectly still
even when the painter cracked

and hurled a stool through the canvas
and stormed off, cursing.

The frame was OK.
He propped it in the garden.

Sometimes he sat in it,
more often not.

*

Why do I tolerate that face?
The liver-spots are droppings on a stone.
Soon my only hairs will be in my nostrils.

I am becoming an embarrassment.
This morning my reflection in the mirror
turned and walked away.

*

Bound in pigskin, tooled in gold,
the collected works: his slightest mumblings,
all his chance asides, marshalled in rows.

It was terrible. That night, like bats
in the thatch, his million words
cheeped and whined in their confinement.

He could not sleep or eat. At last
he flung it in the yard. The pig ate it.
Pigs have no finer feelings.

Later that day
he caught the pig and roasted it
and it fed the whole village.

Time Out

There's a curt breeze up.
A grainy whiteness
far out. One gull looking for its shadow
on a mile of sand. And you,
how strange, it's you.

White wrought iron chairs
are leaning, elbows on their tables.
All the parasols are down
but one. It hackles and slaps
above you. You're taking your ease

deep out of any season
in that bleached-out frock,
arms bare,
leaning back like a lady of leisure.
You ought to be chilled to the bone.

To a life
spent doling cups of kindness!
Now you drink, disgracefully, alone
taking clear water straight on the rocks.
The glass sweats with the cold.

The wind is impatient.
It wants to sweep under our feet.
You won't be hurried now.
A newspaper peels itself page
by page, and every one is white.

What news? There's silence in it.

Broken Images: A Triptych

I. A BEAUTY

Don't breathe! she whispers. *Look!*

The slim trout quivers
in the mill-race as if charged

by the force of her gaze.
A beauty, I have to admit

but I won't, like a kid
in the street who scowls and gapes

outside glittering windows. *Hush*,
the doors sigh; those within

are bathed in a rich light,
double-glazed with wonder;

he can see their lips move
slightly; they are served.

His fingers itch.
He wants to smash and grab.

I want to throw a stone.

2. NOT A SPARROW

There was a sweetness of cut daffodils
like faint reproach.
The tall west window hoarded blues and golds.

Then a piece of the shadows broke loose.
It chucked itself, smack,
at where the glass glowed brightest,

again and again, like the scratch
for a God-awful itch.
In its own world of light

the image of a dove went on
descending with its message
for a saint so practised, so complete

what could surprise him? Real
feathers fell:
the bird beat itself ragged

rather than accept the fact
of glass. *More bloody mess!*
The caretaker looked in: *Me,*

I'd shoot the little buggers . . . but
for Him. The vicar, that is . . .
I'd have passed him the gun

and yet half hoped he'd miss
and take out a pane.
To see a dumb soul make its break?

Or to close my eyes and feel
the fresh edge of a broken image?
(Gingerly . . . It might draw blood.)

3. MERMAID, ZENNOR CHURCH

She's not coy,
slipping out of her scales.
She peels them down like tights

just so far.
Where the first tweak of hair
might be, they ruck and cling.

She shows herself
simply, like the highest mathematics,
an elegant paradox, QED,

in wood that's charred
as if fresh from the stake. Still,
the just-risen swell of her belly

comes out whole.
It's smooth, worn smooth: I'm not
the only one who's had to touch

and touch again,
a bit shy, to be caught kneeling
by the granite altar. Squeamish, too:

what if my fingers brushed
against the scar-grain of a face
that's gone? Those four straight slashes

scored through breasts
and forehead, cheek and chin? Yes,
touch there. Gently. Pray for something

to begin to heal, in me.

A Dangerous Age

He lifts up her face and she lets him,
she lets him smooth it
like a finely rumpled sheet,

stroking out from the eyes,
their dusty corners, down the cheek,
easing ten years away

for a moment. Forking lifelines wait
in the grain of the skin
as if scribed by a 5H pencil.

Rub gently, rub hard; held to the light
the traces show.
It's a dangerous age.

No wonder our grandmothers taught us
to put it away
like their guests-only china

so fine it held shadows. Not old
but not young, these two
tread the cusp, a narrow bridge

without a handrail, breathing quick
from the risk like thinned air,
touching at a time like this

just to steady themselves,
for safety,
though they know there's no such thing.

Static

A rip of tiny lightning in a darkened room.
Her back's torque tensed to slip

a nylon sweater . . . How could he
not touch? The same random electricity

is jizzling on her skin and his.
Now it arcs, a whip-flick

like the moment they first spoke,
that sent him home stung, wondering

where he'd been hit,
like a witchfinder with his needle inch-

by-inching for the damned spot
on himself, inevitably finding it.

Picture Window

Looking out at the drop,
weed-gardens like a green sea-swell,
   he wonders how
young seagulls launch off
right first time or never.

But he doesn't say that.
If the town downed tools
   and looked up now
it would catch them framed
in her window, next to the sky

that is bright and vacant,
waiting for a word. '*Balloons . . .*'
   She's had this dream.
'*There were hundreds, out there.*'
She's got his vision prickling

with drifting exclamation marks,
blots and spatters of colour
   that are, or seem,
scattered spores of a puff-
ball of joy that's burst, just

out of sight. '*One crashed.*
There was a house on fire, kids
    crying in the smoke.'
He thinks of a night of balloons
he saw tethered – how they jostled,

sagged and flared, for charity.
But he doesn't say that.
    He makes a joke.
Hot air . . . They turn away.
Later his wife will sniff his hair

twice: what's that smell of burning?

Night Doubles

On the outskirts of somewhere bypassed in the night
    there's a fridge-blue cube of floodlight

with a high wire fence to hold it in. Matched pairs
    in white kit flicker in the charmed square

like aquarium fish twitching up to a sifting
    of feed. Now they're still; women

menace the net. One man coils for the serve
    that springs them all. They have several

shadows each, that shrink in just to splinter away
    as they leap. Outside the game

tonight, I can't help gazing in. It jiggles us.
    We fall together, or apart, like dice.

Digital

Prescribe me *digitalis*
when the heart beats faster
as with fancying you, or fear,

or the sight of time
dealt in a straight flush
on a watch that's not a face

but a rear-view mirror,
signs and white lines,
tracer flashes shortening away,

that's the bulletproof glass
behind which the bank girl
licks her fingers,

strokes the wad and counts
me out. There's no tick
at the bedside these nights

but green stick figures
try out all
the postures one by one.

They're teaching us to see
ourselves as liquid crystal,
like the grid of a city by night

seen from a mile up,
where streets come alive
at a click of a time-switch,

contact made, your finger-tip
against my thigh.
Outside,

quite close this time,
a siren dopplers by.

Out There

Now this comes back, from nowhere,
like an unsigned postcard: snow
on a hill that cold-shouldered the town,
and tracks, our tracks, not close

or quite parallel, edging together
at last in a wood,
a clearing like a room
with the blinds drawn and furniture draped.

There were ashes trodden into mud
like cooled volcano slurry,
someone's fire. A strand of smoke
spooled up like milk in water.

When I flushed a flame
from cover in the cinders,
it was pale
as something born too soon.

It had been keeping for the night.
You stayed deep in the folds of your coat.
I turned to say *We should be going*,
but, just for a moment,

could not think which way was home.

Serpentine

Every shop in the village is rich with it:
rock bruised green and garnet, lathe-turned
    lighthouse lingams
etched with GREETINGS FROM THE LIZARD.
How's that for our bedside table: a lamp
    with a bulb in its glans?

Some even flash. Fancy, night after night,
the same *Me-again* call-sign . . .
    Or like S in Morse,
Marconi's first wriggle of blips
from a hut on these cliffs, a single letter
    home across

the Atlantic, might it wake a crackling
membrane, like my fingers working snake-
    wise down your spine,
from nape to crease, till I can't tell
which of the skins we slough together
    had been yours, which mine?

Bodily Fluids

That's autopsy language.
It means you and me.

It means holding each other
carefully, at finger's-length,

like tall flasks that might spill.
And what price now, that dream

where we meet like an incoming tide
at the river's mouth, salt-

water tangling with sweet?
I think of sweat-

marked costas,
a tidewrack of discos and bars

where last night's love
is a specimen bagged on the beach;

and I think of the monk
who meditated on his body's

entrances and exits – nine,
each with its own secretion;

and of breath-prints on the window
where we looked out at the rain;

and of a world where bodies heat
to melting but can't touch.

I think, we've got to think.
But not too much.

The Wolfboy's Progress

good

boy

the Professor says
good

(with his back to the locked door)

that's a
good boy

a voice like the tug of a leash

that I might even learn to call 'kind'

one day

            *

the woods have gone slurried
with rain on the window
in here it's all straight lines and rules

the Professor
keeps a black and white world in a book
he spells it out

T – R – E – E
I look away
he can't fool me

                    *

grace, Professor.
that's the state I'm in.
        you want it so,

watching me hungrily
watching as a glossy earwig
        jinks across the table

and *Civilisation*
(did you know you mutter
        as you write?)

deprives us of the taste
for simple wonder . . . true.
        I pick it up at one
        gulp. munch.

                    *

on the red leather sofa
lolls the smug dog. I crouch on the floor,

the only one
she doesn't bounce to. she looks down

down on me with those dim eyes
they call trusting. her no-nonsense nose

is sharp as a sharpened pencil, always
testing.

                    *

what you
don't know, Professor
Know-it-all, is I
can talk.

well, I've got to keep one
secret up my sleeve,
since sleeves
are compulsory here

like porridge
and sour soap. teach on,
I won't repeat a syllable
till the day I say it,

right out —
                'Liberty!'
then who'll be speechless,
eh? but
not yet. not just yet.

                    *

once more, inside me, dress rehearsal: *I
DEMAND . . . (yes) I DEMAND
MY RIGHTS!* today

we have visitors, two stiff ladies
he leads hushily
across the wide carpet

(leaving shadows in the pile
like wind in wheat)
to where

I sit waiting.
now!
'I

DUM . . .
I . . .'
'm dumb. sprung

to a crouch,
I send the hard chair clattering
and all they do

is stare, concerned,
two dried old seedpods
rustling slightly.

the Professor
looks on, taking
notes, professional.

*

shredded blankets
      make a nest
crud-flakes clothe
      its nakedness

chews its hunger
      bitter grub
kips on soreboards
      there's the rub

snarls at pity
      dumb thing lies
gentle gaolers
      damn your eyes!

                    *

free! out
on my all fours
running . . .
                  no.

stop. stage fright.
moon
shadow points me backwards.

busted window
streaks another shadow on.
can't choose

or move. I want to lose
both, to be all
dark in the woods

beyond the wall.

*

the forest won't have me back. I think she's angry.
she wakes me up shivering with the word 'hungry'

on my lips, where before it was simply wanting
as constant as weather. now I'm drawn to
                                        haunting

outskirts. they're so trusting, leaving curtains
open to the dark. they leave their gardens

free for any night-thing to squat and yearn and
                                        stare
in at . . . whatever people do in there.

*

a cat
shrugs itself off its bin,
with bad grace
leaves its pickings to me.
upstairs
a child chafes at a violin.

67

a door
swings, shaking light out
like a tablecloth.
a woman calls. someone
is wanted home.
no answer. I could run

into that life,
those thrilling ordinary
cooking smells,
into someone to be.
and here I go
again, led by the nose . . .

                    *

          trapped, home
     again, Professor, tale
between my legs. I'll lap the gruel

     of each day
in the classroom, fool
among fools who grunt and grope

          for words.
     I'll lick the plate
and beg for more. for you

          I'll grow
     up hard though
scarcely straight or true.

                    *

                    68

Say *ah*.   aaargh
Say *art*.   art?
Tick.   tock tick
Say *arctic*.   cold
Ah tickle.   tee hee
Late.   too late

Once more, together, now:

      ar-tic-u-late.

        *

    and I can sing
words pulled on the string of a tune
like a toy, a wooden duck on wheels
    that clacks and quacks.

    sheet music frightens me
those five-wire fences little notes
swarm up, get snagged and hang on
    twitching to get free.

    I'll settle for Country
and Western, all lonesome and prayery
with coyotes and love, love. oh gimme
    that sweet cringe and whine.

        *

so one day there's this girl
neat

as a clutch of speckled eggs.
I won't break one,

honest. though, oh, I could eat
her up

and her mummy and daddy, her regular bedtimes.
they'd taste sweet,

dry but more-ish, like nougat.
it's only that granny

who gives me an old-fashioned look:
young man

do I know you?
I make them a gift

of my teeth: my most terribly
charming smile.

                    *

last year the werewolf thing was in
        for a month or two. cool
kids rucked up their pelts and paid
        to see me live at the Full
Moon Club. we made the feedback yowl

OK. then word came down the tube:
    this month was eskimo
or pygmy, I forget, and they were gone.
    I stepped out on a cold
cold empty stage and howled . . .

            *

. . . *I WON'T GET CAUGHT AGAIN.*

            *

Memo: get myself a minder
    get myself an agent
    get myself connections
    get a good brief

    make myself a name
    carve a slice of the action
    make myself a killing
    gonna land on my feet

    find myself a sugar mama
    doesn't ask questions
    when I slink back in the morning
    lies and feathers in my teeth

    sharpen up my clause
    and my wits and my pencil
    get ready to pass sentence
    I'll suspend their disbelief

            *

If you could see me now,
Professor . . . Man of letters
to my name. In short,
    I pass

the last test, don't I?
They attend, wine glasses
poised, as I recite
    my party piece.

In the ripple this girl
I'd made a note of turns
her long neck to her beau
    and whispers:

Don't you think he's good
for a . . . Don't you think
he's . . . (reckoning without
    my pricked ears)

      good boy

      good
      boy

      good

Ex

Gusting across, not waiting

for the lights, just one more
loose end of the working day

leaking home through the cracks
in the traffic, at six

already dark . . . Across, between
a humped WIMPEY-jacketed back

hugging two carrier bags
from the off-licence,

and a shock-mascara'd
teenage mum gone grey

in my headlights
(her buggy-bound astronaut

bumping down
to the breath of exhaust on his cheek) . . .

Across, not looking left or right
between the neon CHRIST

IS THE ANSWER on the shut
shop of the chapel

and the Asian minimarket
(the whole family gathered in

round the freezer, disputing,
their faces lit upwards

in Christmas-card glow) . . .
Ghosting across, between

my bumper and the brakelights
of a transit van, not an arm's reach away

and turning for a moment,
square on and not seeing,

it was you —
pale, puffed and bulky

as if flickered up
by my dipped beam out of focus.

I was glad to see you cast a shadow.

Instrumental 1

Play it again.
Sure thing ma'am.
I'll unzip a grin six octaves wide.

See me tickle those ivories
till they hurt. See me rinsing my fingers
in palpable hit. As time goes by

the soundtrack spits and lurches
out of sync. The keyboard ripples
like oiled pectorals while I

(Won't you bend close and whisper
the words in my ear?) mime.
See me mug and smile.

75

The Song of the House

Who'll take these rooms, who'll rake the cinders in my hearth,
    the house said, who can fill me?
I, said the tongue of flame, I'll lick you into shape.
No, said the house, your kind of love would kill me.

I, said the wind, trust me, just leave a little pane
    unlocked, I'll air you through,
I'll blow your memories away. No, said the house,
you'd leave me with no thoughts but thoughts of you.

I, said the rain, I'll stroke you, skin to skin,
    I'll treat you to a grey bouquet
of mould in every room, I'll weep with every crack.
No, said the house, you'd leach my strength away.

I, said the earth, I've waited, waited, wooing you
    with gravity, a love as true as lead,
let go and let me hold you. No, said the house,
nobody gets up smiling from *your* bed.

And then the emptiness walked in, without a word.
    And later we moved in, love, you and I.
There's this place in each other we can't have
or hold: uncurtained windows, hoards of sky.

Instrumental II

The Human Body,
Illustrated –
one to read beneath the sheets . . .

I never reached the rude bits.
I got stuck on diagrams
that flayed us page by page:

the wetsuit of muscles, the veins
like cracks and creepers on a folly,
the worm-casts of gut

and the taut strings of nerves,
this twangling instrument
that's all I've got

to serenade you, like a café gypsy
with no violin
but the bared cords of his arm

as he bobs at your table.
Carves his bow. *Madame*
wants music? The cadenza winces

into, is it
love? as if
it was the one sure thing.

77

I.D.

It's not the bars
of barcode labels,
not those yes/no answers
that add up to who you are.
It's what squinnies through.

It's not the words,
the lines, the printed page.
Caesuras. Hesitations.
That's the shudder of it
rattling the cage.

It's where the record
jumps and sticks.
It's not the notes
whatever their denomination.
It's the watermark that flows

when riffled in the light.
It wears your PIN code
on its forehead like the golem's
holy syllable of life.
Or on its wrist tattooed

like an old flame or shame.
It knows your credit rating,
oh yes, and the name
your lover murmured, once.
It's a dumb clutch of fingers

reaching through the bars for
maybe just the next-door jail . . .
but brushing others, print
to print; they read each other
in the dark, like Braille.

It's hungry, and it starves
itself. It's hungry
to be thin
enough to slip through.
Let it in.

Mispickel

Here's the man, stepping back into daylight.
There's the furnace with its burnt-stone breath.

The hand he holds out is a mitt that grips
and nothing else; he's swaddled up to the slot

where his eyes shift and blink. Now he breathes
almost free. Come payday, that's a bob or two

he'll not say no to. I should leave him
to the facts, statistics settling steady as the smoke

downwind: he won't make thirty. But I see
bare hands, a woman's; quick, her fingertips

unpick him. Unable to do for himself,
he waits; she winds the graveclothes off him.

Strip by strip, skin reappears. He stands
as naked as a thing she's made

and will make, again and again.
His chest is white as cuttlebone,

Mispickel: arsenic ore, reprocessed from the waste of worked-out tin and copper mines.

with scant black hairs and small sores
that don't heal. Half-baked from the ovens,

he has only her to finish him,
quick, while he's back from the dead, on leave.

She rinses, twining fingers in the bowl,
flicking the drops off, while he watches

as if nothing but her touch could make him speak.